Danger & Maddness
A Collection of Poems
By Daniel Gerber and Maddy Jones

Copyright © 2021 Daniel Gerber and Madison Jones

All rights reserved. No part of this book may be reproduced or used in any manner without the prior written permission of the copyright owner,
except for the use of brief quotations in a book review.

Paperback: 978-0-578-95140-9
Lightning Source LLC, 14 Ingram Blvd
La Vergne, TN 37086

www.IngramSpark.com

Index

Contents

Foreword
Danger and Maddness — 2

COMEDY
About A Word — 4
Bacon — 6
Waffles — 7
A Ghost's Addiction — 8
The Poultrygeist — 9
Sonnet IV — 11
The Drink-Off — 12
Slaughter House — 13
My Brand New Girlfriend — 14
Late Night Snack — 16
The Day With No Safety — 18
Hearse-Play — 23
Wishing Star — 25
Little Whore — 26
Interloper — 27
An English Cat — 29
My Dearest Rona — 30
Losing Weight — 32
The Mumbler — 34
The Hermit — 36
Lumpy Charms — 37
Garbage Can Man — 38
Leonid The Giant — 40
Harry — 41
Just Browsing — 42
Butts In the Air — 44
Distraction — 47

ROMANCE
Snapdragon — 49
Rendezvous — 51
Sonnet I — 52
Moonlight — 53
Sonnet VII — 54
Yin — 55

Maddy	56
Glow	57
Blood Red Cerulean	58
Lead Veins	59
Underneath The Moon	61
Sonnet X	62
Brighter Days	63
Dear Loved One	64
Fallen From Grace	65
If	66
Sonnet XI	67
Sonnet XII	68
A Dream Within	69
Sonnet XV	70
On Love	71
Reverence	72
The Intruder	73
The Knot	74

DARK/SERIOUS

Message From Nowhere	76
The Starseed	77
God	78
Get Out	79
Time	80
Solstice	82
Broken Day	83
Waiting	84
I Know	85
Burning Man	86
Nightmare	88
The Spiral Down	89
Scars	90
Windows	91
Alone	92
The Flower Shivers	93
A Mind of Dilemma	94
Sanitized	95
Wicked Clown	96
Cannibal	97
Bigotry	98
I, Demise	100

Sonnet VI	101
No Backbone	102
Eddy Who Comes From Nowhere	103
Outcast	106
Committed	108
Devious	109
Hound of Heaven	111
The Culling Storm	113
Soldier	114
Blood Stain	115
Warrior	116
The Truth of the Man Who's Been There	118
The Cost	119
Sonnet III	120
Fall of a Monarch	121
Sonnet V	122
The Reviled Man	123
Mind, Body, & Troll	124
Beheaded	126
Here I Lie	128
Life Support	129
Indistinct	130
Prayer	134
Dear Sam	135
The Rat	136
Lost Caws	137
I, the Raven	139
Maddness and Danger	145
About The Authors	148

"Imagination is the only weapon in the war against reality."
-Jules de Gaultier

Foreword

In 2020, perhaps the worst year recorded in the authors' lifetimes (knock on wood), wonderful and trying circumstances led ultimately to the uniting of two distinct and equally bizarre authors who decided the best thing they could do in such a time is put out some badass poetry to inspire and delight the world. And so, this twisted sideshow poetry book was born.

It grew up quickly in the suburbs of a uniquely diverse and uniquely poorly known town called Tri-Cities, located in southeastern Washington State. Like many books, it enjoyed laying down, flipping over, and pulling back the covers (how scandalous!), and spent much of its childhood tormenting its family, the neighbors, and the cat (God rest his soul).

After attending college in the 19th dimension, it decided to settle down on a bookshelf, to express its innermost soul to whomever would sit patiently while it performed. It also enjoys red wine and laughter, if anyone will oblige.

The contents of this poetry book are 100% original. The cover is original artwork of both Maddy Jones and Daniel Gerber, and depicts differing takes on the human face: A whimsical eye with a pair of hands belonging to a spirit longing to be free (-M.J.), a bloodshot eye with inner demons tearing themselves out from the inside (-D.G.), A Cheshire Cat grin (-M.J.) and A devil's bleeding smile (-D.G.). *Maddness*, *Danger I*, *Space Maddness,* and *Danger II*, respectively. These capture the essence of the book, as well as the artists, in a mismatch matching of a strange and unusual face.

Danger and Maddness

Herein lies danger,
Ravenous and relentless,
Tearing itself free.

                                        Madness bubbles forth, spilling,
                                            Dripping pandemonium,

Wicked with whimsy,
Wrapping round the broken heart.
Thus, was written down.

                                              Holding pieces entangled,
                                          Rips the soul in twain, mangled

Set loose the madness
That laughs and wails and cries out.
Hold it to the pen.

                                              Words giggling with trauma,
                                            Written pain, joyous drama

A bad joke, a curse,
A maddening catharsis
At its source, danger.

                                            From the heart, in our sadness,
                                            Bound together in madness.

                      -D.G. & M. J

COMEDY

About A Word

I was sitting at a table on a chair inside a room
I was sitting at a table hearing tales of woe and gloom

The light was dim, the air was hot. The things I heard were lousy.
The things I heard upon my chair, they made me very drowsy.
When suddenly my ears pricked up at something that I heard
My ears pricked up upon the simple sound of just one word.

The word was quick and tricky and I almost didn't hear it.
Had I just lost that word I'd heard? I started in to fear it.
But just around the corner stood the word so shy and peeking.
I almost didn't notice 'till the floorboards started creaking.

The word was meek and lonely, but I told it not to fear me.
I leaned over the table and I asked it to come near me.
The word was cautious at the first but as it came grew louder.
It came and stood beside me and it grew so loud and prouder.

I asked it to come home with me, to save me from the gloom,
That simple tricky word I heard inside that dingy room.
Well, late that night when all my trials had tripped me off to bed
That simple tricky word I heard kept playing in my head.

It banged upon my temples like a thunder-storming rain.
It bounced around my face and crown and drove me quite insane.
"Enough!" I cried unto the word. "You're keeping me from sleeping!"
But as I yelled the words big eyes began their watered weeping.

"Oh, no! You tantalizing word. Stop buzzing in my head.
I'm losing sleep and if you do not stop, you'll wind up dead."
My mind was pure exhausted, yet I heard the poor word's sound,
and in a rage, I lost my cool and wrote that poor word down.

I trapped him on the paper but he squirmed and squealed and worse.
He simply wouldn't stop and so I strangled him in verse.
The verse was loose and now the paper shook in agitation.
So, with my pen I pinned it down with nails of punctuation.

At last, the word subsided and my head grew calm and clear.
But when I saw what I had done, I shed a single tear.
I'd strangled, nailed and shut away that simple little word.
It was so mutilated now, how could the thing be heard?

I took the piece of paper to that chair inside the room,
and I stood and spoke the word and told my tale of woe and gloom.

-D.G.

Bacon

Bacon so tasty,
Bacon so meaty,
I eat it so hasty,
Bacon I needy,

Bacon delicious,
Bacon is life,
Cravings are vicious,
Cravings are rife,

I want to eat bacon,
Alllllll day long,
My tastebuds awaken,
Is that so wrong?

Greasy splendor,
I'm in a trance,
Tempting my mouth,
The bacon enchants,

Seducing my tongue,
The bacon sings,
The bacon well-hung,
Hot pleasure it brings.

-M.J.

Waffles

Dread not the despair of mediocrity,
nor the doldrums of the obscure.
Embrace the sweetened certainty
of a never fading joy.

It is square and fluffy and delicious,
the outside slightly crisped.
As you sink your teeth into its unselfish joy,
waves of sumptuous syrup caress your inner cheek
and rapturous delight fills your body to the point of ecstasy.
Fear not its unbridled wonder,
for THAT, ladies and gentlemen, is a waffle.

No longer will I suffer in unending sorrow,
nor bear the burden of an endless night.
I will rise up unto the heavens
and breach the sky!

I will put to rest the bleak and be at peace,
And in the morning, I'm making waffles.

-D.G.

A Ghost's Addiction

'Where has he gone?
Where did he go?
Could it be true?
I just don't know!',

People say this,
When he walks by,
He disappears,
This ghostly guy,

He is a ghost,
It's not an act,
Let's make the most,
Of this strange fact,

The Ghostly Man,
Can walk through walls,
Scare your children,
And pace the halls,

But all he wants,
Is a cup of joe,
If he gets that,
I promise he'll go,

Having no java,
He's brewing up trouble,
Make it hotter than lava!
And make it a double!

-M.J.

The Poultrygeist

My chickens are cooped,
But not for their bond,
They huddle, all grouped,
Fearing something beyond,

In a feathery fright,
They cluck, and they bok,
For they see within sight,
An apparitional cock,

He clucks and he preens,
He's seen, almost naught,
You know what this means,
(And this thickens the plot!)

He squawks and he crows,
Hatching out a big panic,
My chickens are yellow,
And it's becoming Satanic!

His glowing red eyes,
Are really most fowl,
It's better to be wise,
To not look at his scowl,

My chickens all cried,
As he poached with a gaze,
They're eventually fried,
But nary had a glaze,

Disappeared, he's now done,
I'll sneak 'round to inspect,
But I'll grab more than one,
For my dinner to collect.

-M.J.

Sonnet IV

Awaken I, and softly comes the morn
And blink the first and yawn and yawn again,
But feel I agony of slumber torn
That fills my body with a rusted pain.
The Earth forever creeps around the sun
Or rather sun that creeps around the earth
And like the beetle whose life's just begun
The beetle wakes and wonders at its worth.
A never-ness that fills my soul, beckons
To stay in slumber till the body rots,
However, same that soul seems to reckon
To embrace what will be, and not the "nots".
Though pain and sloth against my will do yearn
Arise shall I, and losing sleep I'll learn.

-D.G.

The Drink-Off

He's slim & tall,
With a cowboy hat,
Likes the alcohol,
But naw, never flat,

He drives his ol' truck,
Real late at night,
He goes to the bars,
And picks him a fight,

From fightin' drunks,
He sure gets a thrill,
The way they brawl,
Ain't havin' no skill,

'Til one day, dear Lawd,
The man was dared,
A drink-off was called,
Bad words them two shared,

They drank & drank,
'Til they can't no more,
And the loser, he fell,
Right on the durn floor,

The winner stood up,
The winner he be!
The feller who called
The drink-off, ya'see?

The man who done lose,
Passed out mighty neat,
Next day in the news,
He's a-mugged and a-beat.

-M.J.

Slaughter House

Into the house,
There they go,
Off to get slaughtered,
Off to the show,

Here come the butchers,
That kill the herd,
Oh, for beef's sake,
It's not absurd!

Don't look below,
Just chew on your cud,
My, such a mess,
All of that blood,

'Narrator, Narrator,
I'm soon to be food,
Why are you here,
And being so rude?'

I'm writing a poem,
Describing your fate,
Now, off you go,
Before you're late,

'I'm about to die!
Cut into meat!
You insensitive jerk,
Suck my teat!'

The poem is done,
The cow is dead,
Just like that,
Because I said.

-M.J.

My Brand-New Girlfriend

I'd been single for a day or two,
or three or twelve or years.
It might be that I'm just to strange
or my too large set of ears.

In my loneliness I've searched and tried
but never to success
so much so that I had given up
I was a broken, total mess.

I know what they'd all told me,
that the nice guy never wins,
and so, I built my girlfriend
out of fried potato skins.

I call her Potatania,
the queen of potatoes
for she's not like other girlfriends
Heck, she'll even starch my clothes.

She seems rough around the edges
and comes off crisp, they say
but inside she's simply perfect
in a delicious sort of way.

Her skin is salty on my tongue
in spite of how she looks.
It's what's inside that matters,
though I love the way she cooks.

She oils me up at bedtime,
loves me more than I am worth.
But unlike me she's rooted, man.
She's really down to earth.

She's always packed with energy
and comforts when I'm down.
She doesn't care that I am white,
or that her skin is brown.

Like most, she knows my stomach
is the way unto my heart.
And I'll love and keep her 'till the time
I know we both shall part.

Alas, sweet Potatania,
How you make me feel so full.
You fill that void inside of me
my stomach, heart and soul.

-D.G.

Late Night Snack

Cozy in bed,
Late at night,
Hearing a noise,
He crept in fright,

He bumped into him,
A thief stood there,
Stealing some things,
And thinking it fair,

'Pardon, dear chap,
You steal what I own,
Do you mind leaving?
For this is my home,'

'Sorry, good man,
I'm not yet done,
I need these things,
For I have none,'

The man who sized up
this moonlit marked fool,
Wore a devious smile
With a dripping of drool.

'You should be warned,
You leave my house be,
For I am a cannibal,
My snacks are tasty,'

The thief kept on,
But leapt in pain,
And soon was gone,
But tasted plain,

So do not steal,
For you never know,
Who wants a meal,
and who wants you "To Go."

-M.J.

The Day with No Safety

"'Twas the day with no safety,
And all through the stores
Not a soul was left standing,
Not even Lenore.

No one chose to be safe.
No sir, nobody dared.
Because nobody said so
And nobody cared."
Said the man with report
To his bold supervisor.
A strong supervisor
Of whom none was said wiser.

"Well then, I shall hear
Of the trouble it caused."
"My report," said the man
"Starts with razors and saws."
"Did they cut towards themselves?"
"They all did except Sam,
For he thought he was clever
And cut towards Louanne.

Now for store 63 I am sorry to say
'Twas the only locale
That had worn gloves that day."
"Well, that's great!" Said the supe'
"No, it's not!" Said the man,
"For they wore 'em when sawing
And cut off their hands!"

"Power saws…" Said the supe'

While he shook his sad head.
"We were lucky that only
Three died as they bled."

"Well, that isn't so bad."
The grim supe' then replied.
"Though it feels simply awful
That so many died."

"But sir!" Said the man
"There is more of this sort.
That's just paragraph one
Of my twelve-page report!"
"Oh, dear God!" Said the supe'
With a cringe and a wail.
Who could hardly withstand
The man's terrible tale.

"Oh, please speed this all up
Do it quick for my sake
For I'm simply not sure
How much more I can take."

"Well, the next," said the man
Covers page five through eight,
But believe as I tell you
It is all things but great.
It involves a wet floor
Or well, many you see.
It occurred in store one
Through five hundred and three.
It occurred with a spill,
Well quite many in fact
For the grease bay exploded
And yet no one did act.

So, they slipped in the puddles
In ones and in twos.
They were beaten and broken
And blackened and bruised."

With the look from the supe'
Who seemed sad but confused,
He explained "No wet floor sign
And slick-bottomed shoes.
See the pile was high,
almost straight through the roof."
"Was it really?" He asked.
"Sir, I tell you the truth.

It took fifty-four hours
To clean up the great mess.
But there's more." said the man.
Said the supe' "Oh God Bless!"

"Well, the ladders and forklifts.
'Twas quite a commotion.
As you know you can't stop a lift
Once it's in motion.
The employees were jousting
Their forks through the aisles,
And each great massive crash
Could be heard for a mile.
And they stood on the forks,
And the drivers had phones
And were drinking and driving
With no safety zones.
There was even a forklift
That flew through the air,
And it landed quite safely

In Jessica's hair."

Said the supe' to the man
"Is that all?"
"Well… the ladders…"
"Oh no! I won't hear it at all.
Simply tell me how many
In how many stores.
I have heard of the hurts.
Yes, including Lenore's."

"Well in two thousand stores
With their backs all thrown out
From their lifting, and with all
That I've told you about.
Well, the total is ninety-five."
"Well, that's not so much."
Said the man "That's percent.
Of your staffing and such!
And that's only recordables
The rest weren't so bad.
And I know it's quite awful,
But please don't be mad."

Said the supe' to the man
"I don't know what to do.
It'll cost us six million
Five hundred and two."
"In dollars?"
"In years
To recover this loss!"
"It'll take us that long?!"

"That's the terrible cost
Of a day with no safety.

Oh, the lives and the pain
Oh, I never will want you
To tell me again

Of the people who fell
To the knife and the fork
And the ladder, the lifting
The saws and the work.
Such a day with no safety
But what's sad, now it's ended
Is that all of these things,
They could all be prevented."

-D.G.

Hearse-Play

A man driving around,
Looks nothing awry,
He's seemingly sound,
But let's have a pry:

For the man who drives,
Is commuting a hearse,
Then an officer arrives,
But wait, it gets worse,

The officer commences,
His same ol' drill,
Mentioning offenses,
With the weather quite chill,

The driver remains cool,
Stays collected and calm,
And the cop is a fool,
Charmed out of his qualm,

The man drives away,
And with nary a cost,
To continue his play,
Of lives to be lost,

For the hobby he lusts,
Is the taking of souls,
But first, it's their trust,
Then the bodies he hulls,

After packing the dead,
And working the coffins,
He's roaming ahead,
His slaughters so often,

Surreptitious, he's sly,
You're seeming perplexed,
You don't know when he's nigh,
Could it be you who is next?

-M.J.

Wishing Star

Up in the sky,
A star so bright,
I shall make a wish,
On this cold night,

I wish upon thee,
To laugh and joke,
To live happily,
'Til I'm an old bloke,

How I long to live,
Such a long, dear life,
Free of all chaos,
And free from all strife,

Oh Wishing Star,
How bright above me,
How big you are,
Such a sight to see,

But why are you burning?
And you've gotten so near,
A METEORITE!! RUN!!
IT'S COMING RIGHT HERE!!

-M.J.

Little Whore

The little whore,
Who walks the streets,
She works her charms,
It can't be beat,

The face, the hair,
The skimpy threads,
She tempts the men,
And turn their heads,

I warn you, men,
Beware of this whore,
She's not what she seems,
There is just a bit more,

For under the bra,
That's under the dress,
Replaced with socks,
Is nothingness,

In the panties,
It makes me sick,
Stuffed inside is,
What word to pick…

Don't let her take you,
The way she took me,
For the straight man I am,
A gay man is she.

-M.J.

Interloper

Broken glass against my skin,
torn up sheets. An upturned bed.
Strewn about are shattered peace's
And the demons in my head.

The bedroom is a mess, you see.
The dishes tossed about.
The intruder moved my toothbrush
and consumed all of my stout.

There is evidence all over
Of this never-welcomed sort,
And there's more of it that I could say
To give a full report.

I did not scream. I did not fight,
Nor try to run away
And I did not go confront. Oh no.
Instead, I told her stay.

She broke down the doors and windows
Tore apart the kitchen sink
Knocked down all the walls and paintings
And much more I dare not think.

All the silentness is screaming
And the normal noise is quiet
And inside my head my demons
They've all gathered for a riot.

How she makes me want to Molotov
My normal daily plans
And she stole my sense of comfort
And my Teflon coated pans.

She enrages all my senses
With her moonbeams and her smile
And makes present all past tenses
That I've missed for quite a while

She breaks into all my secrets
Through the walls and through the door
And she holds them oh so gently
For its me she will adore.

Yes, the house is nearly flattened
and her stuff is everywhere
And although she wrecked it thoroughly
I just don't seem to care.

I step over all the messes
Just to hold her in my arms
And I'm somewhat sure that somehow
She won't do me any harm.

She's a welcome strange intruder
And she's broken in my home
And although the place is ruined
Now I'll never be alone.

-D.G.

An English Cat

Stepped on the tail,
Of an English cat,
The kind that wears,
A gentleman's hat,

'Why have you crushed,
The tail on my bum?
Do you have to be told?
That hurts, by gum! '

'I didn't see you,
I'm sorry, dear cat,
Your tail's under m'shoe,
I'm sorry about that'

'That was intentional!
Do not deny!
You did that on purpose,
Then disgustingly lied! '

The gentleman cat,
Not chivalrous now,
Has scratched out my eyes,
But I never saw how,

I have learned my lesson,
To watch where I go,
But now I am blind,
So how will I know?

-M.J.

My Dearest Rona

Oh, they warned us of Corona.
Thought it was some kind of beer...
Said it came over the ocean,
in a panic storm of fear.

We were warned about the wasting
of this callous cough contagion,
and the dark disastrous droplets
that they say can spread the plague in.

It hits one, then two, then twenty,
and there's plenty for the picking
and the numbers rise so rapidly.
The clock is quickly ticking!

So, we keep a social distance,
though its vaster than the ocean,
and we kick ourselves for throwing
out our disinfecting lotion.

We can't go to bars to drink it off,
though bars of soap are game.
Although if you try to drink one
it's just simply not the same...

We're prohibited from public
to prevent this putrid bug,
and we're not allowed to gather.
No! We're not allowed to hug!

It's a vicious and malicious
cross contaminating crazy!
Some of us are getting restless,
some of us are feeling lazy.

Some of us have gone bananas,
mumbling mutters to the ethers
and yet more of us are thanking God
for youtube bluetooth speakers.

Some of us are simply hiding
from those vicious viral vapors,
and yet some of us just want
to buy a roll of toilet paper!

There is nothing much to do
but nothing! Nada! Negatory!
And I guess the point I'm getting to,
with this strange complaining story,

Is it came from o'er the ocean,
Washing right up to the pier!
It could at least have had the decency
to bring along some beer.

-D.G.

Losing Weight

The abuse was bad,
Most mental to me,
The threats and the lies,
That I just couldn't see,

But now I am out,
I'm free, I'm so free,
I'm as happy as ever,
And so many agree,

And now that I'm free,
I mock the abuser,
And what a fatty!
A retarded loser!

This liar, he walks,
With a waddling strut,
And talking the talks
He's pulled from his butt,

The socially awkward,
The pork-bellied jerk,
Will think you are fooled,
With his fake fatty smirk,

He boasts and brags,
To compensate,
For the little he has,
That he uses to mate,

And it's strangely odd,
That his head is so fat,
For it's empty within,
And I lived with that?!

But not anymore,
No, not for me,
I'm happier now,
For now, I am free.

-M.J.

The Mumbler

The misanthropic musings of this masochistic mumbler
are a tantalizing tell-all that he tossed inside a tumbler.
They were crooked callous chaos that will give your mind contusions
and a convolute confusion, masquerading as conclusions.

He besmirches what's bespoken but as butchered blurry bleatings
and makes meanings oft mistaken, so he often suffered beatings.
All he utters under-spoken are unearthly ugly bungles
that, unheard, seem underhanded and untimely verbal jungles.

I was walking with my walk-stick whilst I whiled by the hours
when this mumbler waddled wayward right beside me with a glower.
Then he whispered whistled whimpers, wherewithal I couldn't tell
and his words were subtle slurry, such I almost wished he'd yell.

See, his lips were loose and limber, listing lazy listless labors
and his jiggling jumbled jowls didn't do me any favors.
He was speaking how he started shoveling sandbars with a spoon
but he might have spoke of Satan shoving standards like a loon.

He continued conversation of incessant itching weevils
but I swear he might have spoke of his incest bewitching evils.
I dared not request repeating of his rude repugnant rumbling
nor request reiteration of his badly bungled bumbling.

No, I rapidly retreated to escape this wretched mumbler
but he followed fast with footsteps. Oh, I wished he was a fumbler!
He continued with his mangled mumbled muddled muggy mess
and I cared not what he told me. I was frightened, I confess.

So, he shouted something sour as he spun to sprint away
and he spoke to many others on that dreadful dreary day.
Oh, that mis-beguiling mumbler, now the years are gone, is dead.
Though admittedly I kind of wish I knew just what he said.

-D.G.

The Hermit

'A hermit, I am,
I live on my own,
Here, in my hovel,
I sit on my throne, '

This very old coot,
With nothing to do,
Grabbed all of his loot,
And put on his shoes,

'A walk, I'll take,
It's sunny & bright,
Cheerful & happy,
No reason for fright, '

What little he knew,
A bird was a-wait,
Despising this dude,
And planning with hate,

The hermit left,
And saw, in fright,
A bird attacking,
With all its might,

'Pardon, dear bird,
What have you done?
You've pulled out my hair,
And now I have none! '

'You see, this is why,
A hermit, I be,
Viles, like you,
Have made me flee.'

-M.J.

Lumpy Charms

You lumpish man,
You're jolly & merry,
You're still happy,
Despite what you carry,

You wear a derby,
Atop your head,
Briefcase in hand,
And too well-fed,

Hearty chuckles,
So big & booming,
And a walk-of-waddle,
From lard, assuming,

A forewarning to be made,
About this guy,
Charming are his words,
But lies, all lies!

Keep a close watch,
On that lumpish man,
He, can you, swindle,
With his clever scam.

-M.J.

Garbage Can Man

Here inside my garbage can
I'll never burn, and never tan.
And I'll sit here all day...
Oh look, a crayon!

I'll color a picture in my can.
One of a girl, one of a man.
They cannot smell the sweet garbage;
The smell of puke, and raisin bran.

There is a hole inside my can,
And through it comes both bread and flan.
And paper wads, and dirt and such
It lands inside my garbage can.

I hide inside my garbage can,
This garbage can upon the sand.
It hides me from the light and air,
It hides my crayon girl and man.

I looked at all of them go by,
When in my can was dropped a pie.
A tasty pie to say the least.
I'm in here eating it, but why?

I'm the man in the can.
In the can, the garbage man.
I'm stuck in here because I can.
I can and will, 'cause I fear to grow tan.

Sure, I reek and stink a lot.
Sure, it's icky sticky hot.
But I am scared of what's out there.
And so, I told myself "Why not?"

If you were thin and pale and weak,
If you were labeled as a geek,
You'd join me too inside this can
And we'd become a pair of freaks.

Oh, by the way, if you should stay
I hope you're nice and like to play.
A garbage can man will I be,
Until my stinky dying day.

-D.G.

Leonid The Giant

There once was a man, Leonid,
Standing 8ft tall, how big!
He's a legend, a myth,
And midgets he lifts,
And he's had quite a many side gigs,

He tends on a farm with pigs,
Working himself, with no rigs,
And at 400 pounds,
His stench is profound,
He had smothered the people in town.

-M.J.

Harry

Meet a man,
A man named Harry,
He's in need of a shave,
And it's quite scary,

He's got hair on his chest,
Hair on his back,
Hair on his ass,
And hair in his crack,

He leaves hair on the soap,
Hair in the store,
Hair every place,
From ceiling to floor,

Harry, dear Harry,
Do something, please,
Your hair retains odor,
And you reek of cheese!

Look at your cat,
What will you do?
Your cat's hairballs,
They're the hairs from you!

No hope, it seems,
For your hairiness,
It'll just regrow,
What a terrible mess.

-M.J.

Just Browsing

Bizarre eyebrows,
There's many to find,
The bushy kind wows,
The drawn ones, designed,

But one man stands out,
By connecting his two,
What's this about?
For between them it grew,

His single hair strip,
Brings many to stare,
For the ends have a flip,
And look heavy to wear!

The man has no gloom,
With his bristles of eye,
Employed as a broom,
He'll sweep, it's no lie!

It wiggles with might,
After combing it sleek,
He'll start to take flight,
For his brow is not weak,

He will flutter and flap,
If your kite needs a breeze,
Birds love this ol' chap,
For it's much like the trees!

He can hide things, indeed,
It's nice to have storage,
Can't find what you need?
Well, you'll just have to forage,

No one can brow beat,
His brow well-endowed,
It's hair-raising with feat,
For it's united and proud!

-M.J.

Butts In the Air

In a diamond skinned river,
Caught there, just mid-stream,
All these tufts of white something
Like dollops of cream

They were Ganders and Geese
They were fishing the depths
with their orange seeking beaks
and their downward stretched necks

They were seeking their supper,
A most fabulous fair
Just a gaggle
of butts in the air!

With butts in the air!
With butts in the air!
A most elegant pose
For a fine derriere!
Raising it high without any a care.
Huzzah! With their butts in the air.

The canine, most playful
And wagging its tail
How it longs for the game
How it howls without fail

Oh, it's ready! So ready!
Oh boy! And Oh joy!
It can't wait 'til you throw
Its red squeaky squeak toy!

The dog is stretched downward
And, covered with hair,
Just shaking its butt in the air!

With butts in the air
With butts in the air
A most playful prepped pose
For a fine derriere.
Just wagging it round without any a care
Huzzah! With their butts in the air.

How they dance in the darkness
Igniting the sky
And floating about
As the fireflies fly.

Their rear ends are yellowish
Or maybe they're green
On a warm summer night
Gently wafting, serene.

How your eyes they entrance,
And your romance ensnare,
How they glow, with their butts in the air!

With butts in the air
With butts in the air
A fluorescent fine pose
For a fly'ng derriere.
Riding the breeze without any a care
Huzzah! With their butts in the air.

A sleepy child faceplants
As it lays down to bed
It's simply to tired,

45

To lift its poor head.

It's given up waking.
Its energy spent.
It didn't quite fall down
So, in half it's bent.

At last, it's asleep
With its blanket and bear.
And quite peaceful,
Its butt in the air.

With butts in the air
With butts in the air
A provocative pose
For a fine derriere.
Raising it high without any a care
Huzzah! With their butts in the air.

-D.G.

Distraction

The ticking clock,
The minutes pass,
The old man waits,
And sips on his glass,

He's waiting and waiting,
But what is it for?
He's waiting for Death,
Oh my, it's a bore,

His overlooked name,
On Death's long list,
Was poorly forgotten,
And sloppily missed,

So now the man sits,
At two twenty and three,
He's waiting in silence,
And not happily,

The fault lies with Death,
For distracted, was he,
Upon seeing a nude girl,
Just little ol' me.

-M.J.

ROMANCE

Snapdragon

In the ground, safe and sound,
How you'll grow, grow, grow.
And although I've barely found you
And how little we both know,
From your roots, how you shoot
As your petals grasp the air,
And I watch you grasp at graceful
As the wind blows through your hair.
Not a care, blooming there,
Graceful snapdragon.

All the while as you smile,
With the sun upon your grace,
I can't help but feel imperfect
As we stand here, face to face.
Though I bark, though I bite,
Though I'm known to give a fright
I just want to hold you closely
In the emptiness of night,
Just a hound without sound,
Holding snapdragon

Though you push, though you shove,
Silky as the clouds above,
Softly, kindly, lead me blindly
I can't help but fall in love.
Milky white, sparks of life,
In your soft sweet eyes,
And someday I will impress you
If it takes a thousand tries.
Brilliant white, shining bright,
Lovely snapdragon

Although you are a flower,
And I'm just a lowly hound,
I will strive to gain perfection
For the snapdragon I've found.
Just a hound, ever bound,
Loving snapdragon.

-D.G.

Rendezvous

Bathe with me,
In the sea of stars,
Shimmering beauty,
It would be ours,

Meet me there,
In our beautiful place,
I lovingly dare,
So I'll see your face,

We'd dance in our dream,
A waltz on a cloud,
The moon is a beam,
The nighttime a shroud,

My hand in yours,
Our eyes in a gaze,
Your heart, mine adores,
And in mine, it stays,

Our memories amidst,
How brightly they shine,
But so very missed,
Never real, but still mine,

Our rendezvous dreams,
Will forever go on,
Another world that gleams,
From the heart, never gone.

-M.J.

Sonnet I

So far away, my mistress, far from me
And deepened solitude divides us more.
So that I stand to ope' my arms to thee
Turns fruitless, standing here within my door.
Such distance that I often feel your sight
As eyes of yours gaze from the north upon,
And feel I greater warmth than any light,
that only night reminds me that you're gone.
And as I stand or sit or breathe or pray
I etch the face of you, the dream and hope
That I will see it ere the break of day,
And live I onward bolstered then to cope
For living life from day to night is fine
But living in your love and light; Divine.

-D.G.

Moonlight

I'll be your heart,
Your safest place,
I'll kiss your scars,
Caress your face,

I'll wipe your tears,
All that you've cried,
And calm the fears,
That have you tied,

For I am for you,
However can be,
To be guided through,
To make you happy,

I'll be your moonlight,
When darkness surrounds,
Fighting your nights,
I'm always around,

Your number one star,
To twinkle for you,
To love you lit up,
To heal you anew.

-M.J.

Sonnet VII

Mine eyes do not compare to thee, my love
For in the darkness, they are pained and sore
And cannot seem to find the light above
But lost in wretched darkness they abhor.
It seemed an hour only that I lay
And tried to dream of you inside my head,
But three it was that haunted me that day
With images I cannot shake, but dread.
I pray the pain of waking leave me be
And let me dream of you, whose eyes do shine
A brighter light than seems to shine on me
That bless'ed may I be by sleep divine.
An hour slept, and hour blessed will show
An hour lost to nightmare now must go.

-D.G.

Yin

Will you be dancing with me?
Will you hold me so near?
Your locked eyes may see,
My wistful, nude fear,

Will your heart madly beat,
Upon my embrace?
Or will it slow in defeat,
When I kiss on your face?

Can you feel my soul?
From my touch on your skin?
For the stars are within us,
Our ethereal connection,

You can lead me in dance,
I will go where you are,
I'll show you my romance,
From cliché it is far,

To wholly revere you,
Allaying your pains,
To quelling your hurts,
It is never in vain,

For turmoil has peace,
Both differently strong,
As with love, there is fear,
The Yin to my Yang.

-M.J.

Maddy

What iron fortress or mountain bare
could stand against such illustrious gaze
Oceans swell and rivers flow
but it is in thine azure pools I long to swim
And in those pools of blue would I tread a thousand years
until mine strength wouldst give way
and drowning in your eyes I'd stay.

-D.G.

Glow

The love of my world,
You will always be,
Our hearts in a swirl,
That no one can see,

I'll always love you,
Although we can't cling,
To each other this life,
But our hearts will still sing,

We'll again find each other,
As we have times before,
And love one another,
This life, and many more,

I feel your embrace,
Although we're apart,
Your kiss on my face,
Your love in my heart,

I hope you feel me,
My arms around you,
My kiss on your lips,
My love for you too,

Every night, every day,
Your smile shall glow,
For I'll always be with you,
Despite where we go,

Find comfort in these,
These words I say true,
Dry your tears, please,
My darling, I love you.

-M.J.

Blood Red Cerulean

Not bitter, not sweet,
But exactly in between
Not a spit or spat within it
Though it seems when we begin it
Salivating just to have it
Aromatic and emphatic
Just a taste of you
Blood red cerulean

It flows and falls between us
In a slurry through our lungs
Slowly sung, reverberating,
Glistens bright, intoxicating,
But a drop of you
Blood red cerulean

Ever waft, only gasp
Riddled crimson ever deep,
Venting azure tinted steam,
Take a breath of you
Blood red cerulean

Smooth and silk, soft and hot
Holding beating heart to beat
Hear the drum of you
Blood red cerulean

God and grace, colored face
Catch a glimpse of you
Blood red cerulean

Never more of you
Blood red cerulean

-D.G.

Lead Veins

If you've ever been a part of it
And been there from the start of it
How the lead
From your head
Fills your veins, veins, veins
And once liquid becomes solid
In the heart inside your brain.
Feel the never, never, never
From the love that would but can't
Causing hyperventilation
As you puff and puff and pant.

Yes, I knew her from the start you see
She held my lead filled heart you see.
I'd not know
How it'd grow
In my mind, mind, mind.
And although I knew her little
Fell and faltered in her bind.
For that never, never, never
Was that she was friend, not love.
She will tempt me till forever
With her warm misshapen glove.

For her hand had gripped my heart so fast
I hope it falls apart at last.
Letter sought,
Letter not
No reply, reply.
And the lead inside my mind and soul
Makes me desire to die.
There is never, never, never
As it courses through my veins.

It solidifies and hardens
In my heart inside my brain.

It cannot fall apart at last
It is my body's part and past.
Heavy still,
Hard and ill,
And it's cold, cold, cold.
So, this memory inside of me
Will haunt me till I'm old.
Hear the never, never, never
Of the love I dearly sought
For all emotional pain is
Love that would be, but cannot.

-D.G.

Underneath The Moon

I love the way you care for me,
Underneath the moon,
I love the way you look at me,
From across the room,
In your eyes, I see the stars,
To me, you wish to give,
It's in a place that's near, yet far,
That we'll forever live.

-M.J.

Sonnet X

"Cough Cough" said the man to his darling wife.
Fussing about she went around the house
Looking for a cure to save her man's life
But naught she found but a tiny grey mouse
And so, she wept and moaned for better health
For Husband home and all the air she breathed
That couldn't be bought no matter the wealth.
He coughed and coughed, and then started to heave
And upon the floor a hairball he spat
But breathed he never a clean fresher breath.
His wife nearly fainted and there she sat
With prayer to the lord he'd naught caught his death.
In a might you'll be breathing better air
So, I pray and I'll pray because I care.

-D.G.

Brighter Days

Unsaid words,
Hold such power,
And they get stronger,
With every hour,

Feeling passion,
Feeling disdain,
These are my feelings:
I feel insane,

I'm so confused,
Feeling so numb,
Yet also amused,
Isn't that dumb?

Shades of black,
My world is drab,
Except for a tulip,
That I reach to grab,

So vibrant & fresh,
It brightens my day,
My smile came back,
I hope it'll stay.

-M.J.

Dear Loved One

My dearest loved one,
How clear I perceive you!
Like the light of the sun,
So shining, what is true,

        Like the wind you are chilly,
        Cold and quite pushy,
        Like the waters' depths,
        You surround and consume me,

                Like how bacteria rejoice,
                You cause an infection,
                Like the crackle in a voice,
                You mutilate inflection,

                        Like the bite of a flame,
                        You gave me a welt,
                        And now I douse you,
                        With all that you've dealt.

        -M.J.

Fallen From Grace

Graceful is love, so loving and grasping.
Gilded and gliding and falling so freely.
With uncertain gracefulness,
Love becomes gracile,
Graceless and gliding and falling so freely.
The gracile tumbles and trips.
While tumbling tripped,
And once tripped, love tumbles down gracelessly.

-D.G.

If

If our love is so wrong,
May we never be right,
If our love can't have peace,
Then for it, we'll fight,

If our love is insane,
Then let us stay mad,
If we're causing them pain,
Let's torture them bad,

If our love is disgusting,
Then let's make them ill,
For our loving each other,
Is beautiful still,

If our love is a fire,
We'll burn it all down,
If our love is an ocean,
Together we'll drown,

If our love is the sun,
May it give them a burn,
If our love turns to ashes,
Let us love in our urn,

If our love is the moon,
Let us always meet there,
And if we're both loons,
My love, don't despair.

-M.J.

Sonnet XI

To speak a word of all that I would feel
Would break the will of any less a soul
That the mind itself would flake and would peel
Leaving nothing in its wake but a hole.
I speak of your soul, how it's mixed in mine
Between the ethers that our love will bring
That ne'er be expressed in rhythm or rhyme
But if the worst of all would, it would sting.
Like apart two webs to be ripped away
That were sewn apart, but brought together
Then neither being whole, would stand or stay
Being better off if had they never
My soul, with yours entangled, and smitten;
Given choice o' the bug, better off bitten.

-D.G.

Sonnet XII

In pain and sadness often do I sink
To depths below the lowest pit of hell.
It fills my mind with all the sulf'rous stink.
With all my might I only wish to tell
A truth that sings above the clouded sky
In sunlight doth alone it bathe and bask,
I wish to trust the beauty in mine eye
Whose rosen lips, of me, their trust, they ask
That I may rest with truth I cannot doubt.
I shall bend to hold your honor high;
To pass above the demons I shall shout
"She is as true as heaven, declare I!"
I know my mind doth break and boil and bend.
It is your patience with me that doth mend.

-D.G.

A Dream Within

I had a dream,
And you were there,
So real it seemed,
And without a care,

To me you confessed,
Your feelings unknown,
There was nothing to guess,
Of the love you had shown,

And then I awaken,
From the dream within,
But I was not shaken,
For I woke with a grin,

And then I see you,
And how you see me,
But I wonder your view,
In this reality?

-M.J.

Sonnet XV

Shaken softly by a glare of thy soul
The green lights my heart and shudders it all,
That falters over tongue and step and stroll
Wafting, gliding, but in thine eyes I fall.
I never thought a green like those could make
A man quiver and shy away in fear
And countless breaths from without my lungs take
As standing breaks my nerves when thou art near.
Confusing thoughts, though careful, meet my gaze,
Like warnings do you sometimes slip my way
As if to say "I'll break it fifty ways"
To heart of mine, but wonder I away.
I cannot think but into emerald eyes
Wherein, I fear, now broken, my heart lies.

-D.G.

On Love

The calm after storms,
The quiet after rain,
The peace of a rhythm
That resounds in the bones.

Play it louder, let it grow,
Fill the sorrow with release.
Resonate in the hollows
Fill the void with its sound.

Shining lights, a cacophony
Beats hard in the skull
A torrent of sounds and screams
A torch burning hot in the storm.

Love is a tide, slipping away,
Fading, receding in quietest night,
Let it fade, let it burn out,
and bring me the dawn,
That I may await the next song to be sung.

-D.G.

Reverence

My heart is at home in your hands,
I feel at home in your arms,
Relief wafts over and lands,
Completely succumbed to your charms,
Your spirit, enticing and gentle,
Has always caressed upon mine,
Quenching my fears, how tranquil,
As though it's the finest of wine,
Our lips, so tender with rev'rence,
Warmed with our shared esteem,
When they touch with a powerful suff'rance,
Affections composed like a dream.

-M.J.

The Intruder

A broken lock and window found I there
When I, unto my home, returned that night.
And finding scattered rocks upon the stair
And hearing creak and groan, I took a fright.
Disheveled all, possessions of my heart
That groaning devils revel in my head,
That keep the rotting corpse that is my part,
And finding there within an upturned bed.
My peace was ripped away with but a glance
And home had changed to hovel in its turn.
The Intruder had upon me snatched my chance
To live serene, and forced my soul to burn.
Found I within my home expressions lewd,
And blasted all, when my love did intrude.

For all the wants and wasted years gone by
And habits formed now dashed away in spite,
This ne'er-do-well the curtains ripped awry.
Affections hers, have filled this hall with light.
My broken lock and window now are gone
And with them all the groaning devils fled.
The rotting corpse now filled with life, lives on
And She, intruder graceful, fills my head.
Never a gentler prowler have I seen,
That through my windows stole upon my soul.
Like muse to my poet heart doth she mean
To inspire. Softly then she makes me whole.
This woman turns me, to gold from pewter
And in my heart a welcome intruder.

-D.G.

The Knot

Some knots are meant to tie things up
Some knots are meant to bind
Some knots are made to be undone
and some are left behind.

It simply wouldn't serve you see
To pull these two apart.
This knot is not tied up with strings
Instead, it's tied with hearts.

Try not to pull it to the left
Or push it to the right
Or pull it sev'ral diff'rent ways
And tie it up too tight.

For it's not one string, no, but two
That tied themselves together.
A strong and bonded tied up thing
Most difficult to sever.

'Tis such a precious thing you have
So, tie it up with extra care
And don't forget ye knot that stands
For all the love you share

So, when you've tried and tied it up
With all the strength you've got
And wonder if it's made to end
Remember that it's knot.

-D.G.

DARK/SERIOUS

Message From Nowhere

This message comes from Nowhere
and from nowhere in between
and once you've been you'll know it
just exactly what I mean.

There's a river and a shiver
and a sliver down the lane.
There's the pain that makes you bitter
and the joy that keeps you sane.
There's no rhythm, rhyme, nor reason,
no preoccupation there.
There's no tender love to hold you
and there's nobody to care.
You won't find a moral standpoint.
No one has one anyway,
As they all parade around you
in the darkness of the day.

It's a simple little village,
town or city, burg or port.
It has buildings, plains and chasms
to confound as you contort.
With your face all screwed in tension
at the anger that you feel,
you will wonder "Will they listen?
Will they harken? Will I heal?

There's a mailbox in nowhere.
It is round and square and tin.
People wonder at its contents,
and the words that lie within.
It's a simple solemn Nowhere.
It is soft, and rough and mean.
And it's where this message comes from
and from nowhere in between.

-D.G.

The Starseed

I come from the stars,
Or maybe from mars,
To heal the afflicted,
The hurt and constricted,

Heavy hearts of the sad,
The insanity of the mad,
I've come to help you,
Feel alive and anew,

I will help you along,
To be singing your song,
As you were meant to do,
As you feel it is true,

I will give you my light,
There's no need for fright,
But you know that I'm rare,
For I came from out there.

-M.J.

God

In amid the fighting and turmoil,
the struggle and shouting and gnashing teeth
a moment is taken, where the roar is soft and silent
and the torrent of wind and debris dies down.
I find comfort there, as I take a breath of creation
and allow myself to be in God's presence for a change.
Like a mother, I feel her come to me full of understanding
Like a lover, she holds me, her soft hand upon my face
A smell of soft lilac as I lay beside her
and she whispers to me "it's okay."
She holds me as long as I desire, and does not change.
No tear is judged, not a word is spoken
and for a time, the broken screaming of the world
is no more than the whispering of the breeze.

-D.G.

Get Out

I gotta get out,
No one hears me,
Whenever I shout,
No one hears me,

I'm isolated,
I'm all alone,
But I'm being haunted,
While you're gone,

My life is done,
I've had enough,
I'm too alone,
It's been too rough,

I gotta get away,
There's no escape,
No one wants me to stay,
Uncontrollable hate.

-M.J.

Time

If time is linear
Why do we measure it in circles?

Seconds go round, their contribution so minute
Yet the make up a minute

And Minutes go round at sixty miles an hour
But then they're right back where they started.

Days turn to nights turn to days,
And when you add them all up, we start again at 1

Months pass by and each one is special,
But isn't special unique? I've seen how many January's?

Years go by and at first, we're all excited
Because it's one, two, three
But now we're thirty, forty, fifty
And we really wish they'd just stop.

In thousands of years, we've thrown out all the calendars.
What year is it, really?

I used to watch the stars as they passed overhead to who knows where.
Now they're back and we haven't moved.
We're running around in circles convinced we're moving up
But no matter how tall the helix gets it still hasn't moved forward.

It's no wonder all the politics and social warrior justice,
God fearing murder and unending warfare haven't gotten us anywhere.
We're just spinning our wheels and going around in circles.

There's got to be another way to do this.
Something else we might try instead.
Let's set our path straight instead of in circles.
Maybe it's time.

-D.G.

Solstice

The warm wafting breeze rests against my skin
and cracks the branches of ancient trees
like memories; sharp and hollow
Our summers dry out the past and leave us longing,
aching
reaching down just to touch our toes
in the hopes that the past will be bright and full once more
Hot winds blow them around like the dust
and we try to grasp them in our hands.
We can't go back anymore. Not you, nor I.
All we can do is make a choice:
Do we hold on to those memories like the hollow shells of insects,
or do we let them fall to the ground like so much dust?
I don't think there's a way to truly let them go,
they lean against us like so much breeze;
Warm and comforting but impossible to hold.
You know as well as I that to lay in them is to die in peace
but trying to erase the wind completely is foolish.
What then?
Will our memories fade as we leave them on the road,
or do we spend our days listening as they whisper through the trees?

-D.G.

Broken Day

It's just another broken day
Where discord chants ere it's begun
To hear the mournful hellhounds bay.
Each step begets a deep dismay
No battle this way can be won
It's just another broken day.

Wretched path on which you stray.
Likewise, strangers it will shun
To hear the mournful hellhounds bay.
Before you woke, 'twas cold and gray
No promise of the shade or sun
It's just another broken day.

Bleak and dreary, darkened gray,
Rends you hollow, nothing, none,
To hear the mournful hellhounds bay.
Fear belies, desires play.
Desires lost in fear undone.
It's just another broken day
To hear the mournful hellhounds bay.

-D.G.

Waiting

Every night, and every day,
There's a man who waits to die,
Frail and thin, wrinkled and gray,
The waiting feels heavy to sigh,

Too slow to die, too slow to live,
Waiting for his time to end,
Only hugs, has he left to give,
For as long as time will lend,

He's too tired to continue,
In misery and pain,
But he keeps on waiting,
No release yet to gain,

He cries with his plight,
But with tears that are gone,
There's no more to fight,
How long? Oh, how long?

-M.J.

I Know

I held your hand to comfort you,
And said you'll be okay,
My eyes held yours to show you this,
And I continued to say,

That even in the end of things,
Still, you'll be okay,
You held my gaze,
Right where you lay,

Then spoke a potent phrase,
With your words so slow,
In your final days,
You simply said "I know."

-M.J.

Burning Man

Ignite.
Ignite.
In the shadows, burning bright.
Like a silent orange projection
softly playing in the night.
How it cloaks him, how it chokes him,
all the little things unspoken
all the things he'd badly broken
all the blame within his sight.

Bitter sweet
Incomplete
burning embers at his feet.
As the memories become a blaze
of follies and deceit.
All the words he spoke and things he said
the shame he feels within his head
each tender wound he knows he's made
engulfs him in its heat.

The words he wishes to withdraw,
all he wished they never saw
cannot change
or rearrange,
Cannot bend or break or leave.
Ev'ry memory or enemy
or sight or sound that tends to be
within each present memory
seems all the more deranged.

Glowing still
Ever real.

The immolation swells until...
'til it catches ev'ry crevice
ev'ry corner of his thoughts.
Ev'ry sentence, ev'ry gesture
fills with boiling fuming pressure
and erupts into a fissure
burning searing fiery hot.

Blazing white
fills his sight
ev'ry vision passing by.
If he could forget the past he'd made
he'd tear it from his eye.
If he knew that he'd mistaken
what within he thought they'd taken
he'd forgive all of the breaking
Though the fire is burning bright.

Let it snuff
let it fade
'twas himself he had betrayed.
Now with sorrow dies the fire
he alone now knew he'd made.
'Twas so long ago to him it seemed,
his heart was light and sound and whole.
Now ashen wounds upon his bones,
and scorches on his soul.
As the smokey column rolls,
and after all the things unfolded
and the embers grow cold,
the story told,
of the burning man.

-D.G.

Nightmare

At twilight's time,
It's time for bed,
It's time to sleep,
So rest your head,

In your bed's warmth,
You shall sleep,
But in your slumber,
You shall weep,

A good dream turns,
A nightmare comes,
A nightmare burns,
A trick is done,

Heart is a-thump,
Enveloped in fear,
Drenched in sweat,
Torture is near,

Swiftly awake,
Calming nerves,
Wipe the sweat,
Repose deserved,

Finding relief,
A nightmare aloof,
Only to find,
It's about to come true.

-M.J.

The Spiral Down

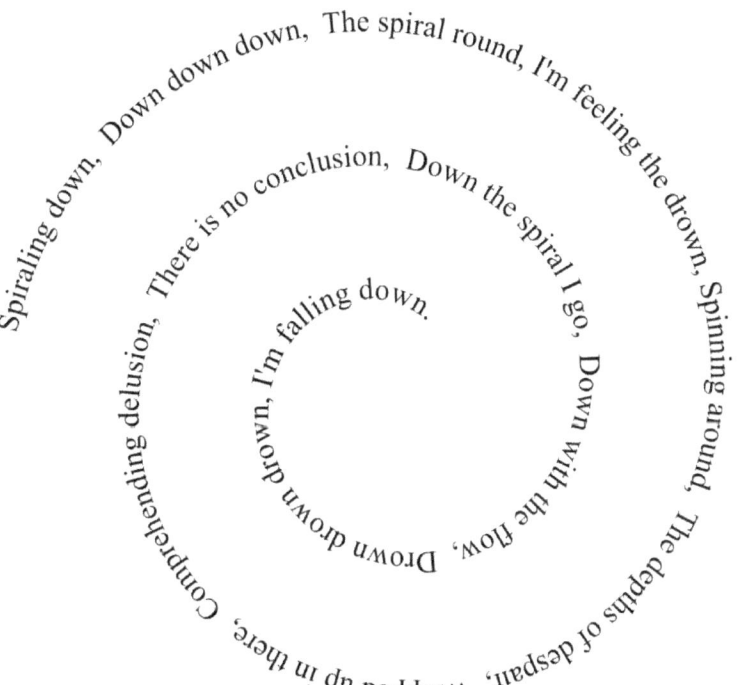

Spiraling down, Down down down down, The spiral round, I'm feeling the drown, Spinning around, The depths of despair, Wrapped up in there, Comprehending delusion, There is no conclusion, Down the spiral I go, Down with the flow, Drown drown drown, I'm falling down.

-M.J.

Scars

Screams as a child,
Fears as an adult,
The tears, they run wild,
And are made of tumult,

The wounds from inside,
Are old and well known,
Her scars that reside,
Have stayed 'til she's grown,

They're haunting,
They're chilling,
They're daunting,
And killing,

Her ebony depths,
The darkest swim,
Has a beautiful end,
Albeit so grim.

-M.J.

Windows

What do you see,
When you peer into my eyes?
Do you see sadness,
Or are you none too wise?

Do you see the pain
That they try to disguise?
Holding back tears,
As if they had ties,

Are they intense,
Vibrant, and wild?
Or maybe they're tame,
Soothing, and mild?

Are they breathing alive,
Or so vapidly dead?
Do they often look down,
Or look up ahead?

Are they warm with heart,
Melting, and tender?
Or do they seem distant,
Like faded splendor?

The windows to the soul,
What do yours say?
And what do you think,
Of my eyes today?

-M.J.

Alone

There's no mercy to the source of loneliness.
No semblance of second chances
Nor the glance of a lover,
not once across the room.
Had I seen ahead,
set a mirror in front
I'd have seen the shadows I carried
and the blackness that clung to my skin.
So hollow now, knowing
that I had one chance at something good.

I blew it.

The fever took me and I gave in
and let the madness of indulgence drive me on
'til the fever raged to such a fury
that it burnt through my very soul.
Now, here I am.
Standing on a cold shore amid the beaten rocks
staring out into a vast ocean, screaming
"I love!
Would that I were loved!"

But the waves do not answer.
They don't listen to my cries.
All I hear is echoes
And the beating of waves against the rocks.
That is how I know loneliness.
It is not a sorrow that fills the soul.
It is a vast emptiness
Stretching endlessly before me,
Where no cry is heard but my own.

-D.G.

The Flower Shivers

The flower withers,
Dying today,
The flower shivers,
Wasting away,

A useless soul,
An early death,
Becoming cold,
A quieted breath,

The flower dries,
The petals fall,
The petals lie,
The living stall,

Death of a cough,
Why thrive on?
You cannot slough,
You cannot run.

-M.J.

A Mind of Dilemma

'Amnesia, amnesia,
Forgetful me,
But who am I?
And where could I be?'

The stranger says,
Moving along,
Passing through,
Guessing wrong,

Checking his clothes,
For clues & such,
But searching in vain,
And having no luck,

With an aching head,
And trembling hands,
He wanders on,
This forgetful man,

The wayward tramp,
Leaving no trail,
Continues his search,
But to no avail,

Poor little man,
He has no clue,
You should be glad,
That this isn't you.

-M.J.

Sanitized

The man in the pit
Alike the man in the cage.
Sour slop smells of shit
And incites his blood to rage.

Today is the Long Shift,
Today is the torment
An endless incessance
Where half a glass is but lament

Working on in the pit,
Soaking scrubbing all away
Scratching porcelain with forks,
Cracked ceramics and decay.

Break time is closing in
But in that space, it piles up,
And the smell of jam is vomit,
And the man has had enough.

He can't stand it, he can't take it
As depression leaves its mark.
Though the stench is never ending
And the white of plates is stark

He, now connoisseur
Of detergent takes a sip.
He won't get back to work.
He's not returning from this trip.

He'll never rip the stench of labor
From the fibers of his clothes.
And the beast within the pit
Is now a beast left in repose.

-D.G.

Wicked Clown

That happy, fun clown,
He's so full of joy,
With giggles and laughs,
From the girls & the boys,

Seemingly fun,
A balloon he'll make,
Whatever you want,
It's yours to take,

How silly is he,
With that red nose,
That white makeup,
And big, bright clothes,

Handing out candy,
That I eagerly ate,
It tasted so dandy,
I regret it to date,

'Twas sharply sweet,
The cries I then sung,
A rarely sliced meat,
I lost my whole tongue,

That wicked clown,
Don't ever trust him,
Hurting for pleasure,
While filling his whim,

So please watch out,
When you get your sweets,
You don't always know
All the tricks in your treat.

-M.J.

Cannibal

Lacking a weapon I wait, I wane.
I sharpen the teeth, I long for the pain.
The bodies around, these fools I detest.
These imbecile infants, I swear I'll digest.
I'll chew up their innards. I'll grind up the rest.
They burn up my patience. My restraint they test.

I cannot hold back, no. I cannot be gentle.
Their unending bullshit drives me simply mental.
Devour the idiots. Digest the dull.
Take no more complacence. Take none of their bull.

I'm a cannibal, ravenous. A cannibal bare.
I'll no more sit idle. I'll no longer care.
I'll eat up their bullshit. I'll eat up their flesh.
I'll silence their stupid. I'll put them to rest.
I'm a cannibal reckless, incensed and enraged.
Put me in the madhouse, put me in the cage.

I can't take much more, love. I cannot hold back.
I long for the end of their infantile snack.
Take heed of my hunger. Take heed of my plight.
I'm the beast that devours and feeds in the night.

I'm a cannibal, sweetheart. A flesh-eating fiend.
You've seen what I long for. You know what I mean.
You know that I seek to devour the dull.
It's the reason I eat. It's the wicked I cull.
I'm a cannibal, hungry, ravenous, bare.
Your love is the reason your life I will spare.

-D.G.

Bigotry

Everyone lives and everyone dies.
Everyone laughs and everyone cries.
Everyone walks in the sand and the dirt.
Everyone loves and everyone hurts.
Everyone on this dear earth is the same.
They have the same laughter,
they share the same pain.
They're all equally blessed
(or else equally cursed)
but there's just one kind
that is known as the worst.

Oh, dear loathsome bigot.
Detestable cur!
The champion of hatred,
the fearful, the sure.
Take heed of this warning:
There's nowhere to run
there's no place I won't find you.
Your time here is done.
For I am the bigot of bigots, you see
my intolerance captures
intolerant thee.
I won't take thy beatings.
I won't take your lies.
I'll look in your ignorant
close-minded eyes
and I'll strike out your legacy
with kindness and strength
You will leave no inheritance.
I'll go to great lengths
to teach well all the ignorant,

strengthen the weak,
humble the prideful
and enhearten the meek.
The age will be made, sir,
with no place for you
so, give up all your nonsense
and search for the true.
Poor, misguided bigot
You will soon gain some worth.
When you give in to those
Who inherit the earth.

-D.G.

I, Demise

Meet your wonder,
Meet your death,
I hold your future,
Your one last breath,

I am grim,
I am just,
I am unfair,
Do not trust,

Dishonesty winds,
The tangles of lust,
Hatred breeds,
From hatred of one,
Upon these conditions,
Sometimes I come,

Sometimes I take,
Sometimes I leave,
Guess who I am,
Will I take thee?

I am dark,
I am cold,
I take strong & weak,
And young & old,

It's my job,
The souls I rob,
What is my name,
When demise is my game?

-M.J.

Sonnet VI

Ay me. That I must go and bust my butt
And stand for an endless time upon feet
That early feel afresh and start to strut
But late become a shock of bone and meat.
Upon such feet I stand again, again,
Entrenched upon a cold and stony floor
And wait for such an end to come of pain
To walk me to a sliding glasséd door.
A day now gone to come again, again
Entrenched, I wait, again it comes anew
But being all the same, not new, but same
As mindless numb pervades the whole day through.
Again, it comes and breaks my spirit whole
Into a million pieces through my sole.

-D.G.

No Backbone

Fire in eyes,
Darkness in mind,
Conscious unwise,
Intentions unkind,

Prompted to take,
Life in its wake,
Slaughtered his own,
Victim unknown,

Sorry, but late,
Inevitable fate,
Soon to succumb,
Victim undone,

Heart of stone,
No backbone,
Ruled by disdain,
Leaving the slain,

No second thought,
Why, why not?
Evil now roams,
For future unknowns.

-M.J.

Eddy Who Comes from Nowhere

Do you see?
It's half past three.
And Eddy who comes from nowhere.

In the street
You just might meet
Eddy who comes from nowhere.

His legs don't pitter
His legs don't patter,
He comes with clank
And clack and clatter.
His legs have braces
Each made of steel
So, hide your faces
And do not kneel
Before Eddy who comes from nowhere.

We do not know
What made him so.
We cannot see
To where he'll go.
But he's Eddy who comes from nowhere.

He came out of
The foggy air
He'll wait for those
Who stop and stare.
He waits for you to view the legs
Of Eddy who comes from nowhere.

And when they stop
They're soon to drop.
Whether they're
Citizen or cop.
One look from him and you'll be killed
By Eddy who comes from nowhere.

It's said that Eddy
Has no gun.
He's got no knife,
And yet we run.

His gaze is what kills you
And it isn't much fun.
Not for Eddy who comes from nowhere.

One fine spring day
I stood in the way
For Eddy who comes from nowhere.

I did not stare.
I did not gawk.
My eyes stood fixed
Just like a hawk.
And when he came, I made a shout
At Eddy who comes from nowhere.

I asked him why
His legs were braced.
I stood and looked him
In the face.
He stood amazed
And met my gaze,
That Eddy that comes from nowhere.

"I've lost my home,
And now I roam.
I've lost my house
And broke my bones."
He stopped and cried
And rubbed his eyes.
Poor Eddy that comes from nowhere.

I took him in,
Gave bread and gin,
To fill out right
That boy so thin.
I did it to see
That he'd no longer be
An Eddy that comes from nowhere.

-D.G.

Outcast

Loneliness echoes, let go.
It shows, the rose and the sneers.
It's weird. Cold and relentless;
Messed up. Enough. A rough ride;
They lied. The masks with no words,
You aren't heard. Absurd. You beg;
To take or make the pain past.

Gray skies all over, they grasp
They make sober. They roast pain
Deranged, in soft rain they play.
You can't stay, so out you call
Through halls of thick concrete walls
That's all. No things you wish were,
But hopes turn to burs and spurs.

No eloquence heard with jokes
That don't laugh. An Epitaph.
That which burns becomes hollow
Now gone lonely to wallow
Longing to break glass and pass
The mass of distance between
The mean eyes. The ties that blind.

It's still. It's empty. It stings
The torment brings the just means;
The furious clutch, as such
You grasp to escape. Mistake.
Words pass fast through glass, besides
It won't break. No friends lost here.
So, take fear, and journey's make.

Left standing alone, the stone
The Cement. The rent that spills,
Brings new faces chills, the friends
Don't end or add up; don't fit.
The pieces rip to black chips.
Wash it clean through to stark white
The rain now flows and takes flight.

The thing spreads wings, it won't sing
It brings a lingering crack
And laughs as you leave, cracked!
Bereaved. It hurts but won't last
You did the sick math, the path
Resolute to outlast it.
    So, long stand the outcast.

                -D.G.

Committed

Thoughts in his head,
Hugging his knees,
Trapped in a room,
Oh, woe is he,

The padded room,
The strapping coat,
All is white,
His mind a-float,

He's simply gone mad,
Crazy, it seems,
He's been committed,
Or so they've deemed,

Sick in the head,
He's not quite right,
Talking of nonsense,
With all his might!

It's pointless for him,
Pills do none,
Talking is futile,
And shock is no fun,

What sad despair,
How feeble, is he,
With no one to care,
Ignoring his plea.

-M.J.

Devious

Broken hearts don't mend they bend
They break into piles of teeth
Beneath the silk skin within.
So, it begins the sick grin
To find the cage, greet the rage
That beastly now breaks. It aches.
The mistake makes furious.

Lessons learned won't teach, they burn
And spurn the vicious savage
To ravage, to rip, to tear,
To care about the others
Who won't care for you a scratch.
So harrowed, howl. Bark and growl.
They're foul. You're precarious.

In frightful scene, be kind, but mean.
Obscene with sweet violence
That reaches out, tears, and swears.
Unfair that benevolence,
In reverence, swims and swells.
It tells the sick cells to fight.
The blight rights the spitefulness.

No harm intended, but mend
And make sacred. Be naked
And cry 'havoc'. Cry sweet pain
And rain to wash away, but stay
Fierce. Now pierce hearts with anger
But linger on the insight
That rights, without influence.

For you the grass sways, but prays
To stay solid. Methodic
Sweet stains will fleck grains and brains,
But pain sticks and dries. Besides
The flight dies. The birds cry out.
They shout in protestation.
So, roar loud and glorious.

The sick song bays loud and long.
The wrongs turn intent, and meant
To revert, the hard and hurt,
To dirt. A brutal boot stomp,
A rough romp, the chomp. Meat's tough
But it's enough. But just watch.
Love froths and smells bloodthirsty

The red slur, the scratch and fur
That blurs. It won't harm, but arms.
It's intense, glows and repents.
It's dense and feels numb,
Becomes accumulation
Of all pain felt previous.
      It's Devious

                        -D.G.

Hound of Heaven

I the seething hound of heaven
Sent to hell and charcoal savors
Hellish bound sans blood or brethren
Labor long for something sweet

I the blackened hound of heathen
Breathing heavily and drooling
Dream of reddened; breathing,
Drooling, longing for the scent of meat

I the hound of heaven
Dreaming, screaming for plush and luscious meat

By the angels, I appointed
Sit and obey god's command
Though my orders seem disjointed
Here I sit on blackened sand

Grinding 'neathe my feet and paws
The blood and blackened mud and sand

At the gate of wicked wishes
I await no boar nor fishes
In my stagnant, sentry bring me
Dishes, steaming sinners sweet
Bring them chopped and stewing sweet

To my iron gates of glory
Bring me sinners fresh to eat

Let their souls be bare and bloodied
With sweet juices sweetly running
Let their souls be kept un-muddied
Lest my cunning cutlets taint

Taint my tongue with torpid taste
Ere my taste buds go to waste

To my gate go base and bastard
Sins of sex they've met and mastered
Murder, lies yet faster
Come the bastards to portentous gate
Let the monsters meet their fate

Midst my gums they glom and gather
In my maw their juices splatter
Like a gushing fountain, sloshing
Neither washed or wasted flesh

As I chew the charred and callous
Savor malice, hate and anger
Without cup or chalice spill the
Altruistic hearts of men
Savor, I, the sins again

Give, I, punishment or pleasure
While I feast on human horrors
Human flesh I taste and treasure
Sinners all to me are led

Sit and wait for supper, to be,
I, the hound of heaven, fed.

-D.G.

The Culling Storm

Tossed about,
In the waves of her sorrow,
Swimming throughout,
Life's only to borrow,

Abused and weak,
He's given her fright,
Her hope is so bleak,
With no end in sight,

His hatred untold,
A venomous storm,
She's getting so cold,
And cannot stay warm,

Disturber of peace,
And hateful of souls,
He wants her to cease,
And many he culls,

Sinking down deep,
Down where its dim,
Its peaceful to sleep,
But staying is grim,

Her little last hope,
The fins on her tail,
Her gills to breathe,
Oh, who will prevail?

-M.J.

Soldier

We stumble and stomp,
Though branches break
And slide through the mud
Soaked and stinking.

The vines and slime,
How they grow and gripe,
But shield us all
In the moist maze.

We slap and slash
Through green and brown.
Toting guns,
We gamble with green lives.

What are we here?
The stench and sweat?
A vomit of olive-green patches?
We are sick.

We defined this
An emerald in the east,
We rip and tear green
That may not grow again.

-D.G.

Blood Stain

Hidden in the brush,
Heavy silence, heavy stealth.
You're hiding from Heathens,
Hiding from Heaven and Hell.
The blood beneath burns. It soaks your soul.
Soaking your knees, you kneel in it.
Your heart remembers the heathen act.
The moment you hacked and hated.
Halting your enemy with slash and stab.

The halberd in your hand half-soaked in sin.
The chasm between your heart and Saxon souls
Bridged by the hack and torn by the heart.
You hold all remains of him within your tunic,
The twine and weave you wear. Holding the blood, the soul
That's tipped and tainted the halberd in your hand.

You're hiding from heaven in that brush and briar,
Afraid of the heavens forbidding you harmony.
Hiding from hell in that blood and fire,
Afraid of the devil condemning you whole.

-D.G.

Warrior

Comes the woman from the mountain,
To the sand and earth she kneels,
With a mind as soft as raindrops
And a gaze as hard as steel.

Knowing death, Ev'ry breath
Fearing only her defeat
Though the earth might pull asunder
All the ground beneath her feet.

Her foes aren't men, but madness
And her struggle: not but pain
Though she relishes it not she knows
It's now, or not again.

Ev'ry step, Ev'ry strike
Ev'ry tear she never shed
Each and ev'ry one a soldier
In the war inside her head.

With her mind made up to carry
All the burden that she fears,
Feels the rumblings of the war drums
Slowly rising in her ears

Not in strength, not in peace
Not in blade or bow or shield
Not to anyone she knows,
Yet to herself she cannot yield

Dancing like the gentle warrior
Who knows the fight won't end,
She takes up the sword to carry on
'Till battered heart doth rend.

Broken will, Broken heart
Broken spirit; severed all.
Though her legs and wings are broken
Even still, she doesn't fall.

What it means to win the battle
For the heart and for the soul,
Surviving shattered bones that rattle
And a body never whole.

Comes the woman from the mountain
Fighting tooth and claw to dream,
Standing 'lone upon the earth and sand
And in that place, serene.

-D.G.

The Truth of the Man Who's Been There

Once you're a man, the world is defined.
Once you're a man, your world is stale.
In truth there's nothing more to see.
In truth it's a sad tale.

You talk of how you've been there,
You walk as though you've been there.
So, share it all, you man among men,
Share all the things you say you've been.

You know all that you dared to learn
In spite of all, and it's their turn.
Once you're a man, you claim you know
Once you're a man, you've just one view.

In truth your speech is hollow,
Knowing only what you dared to do.
But once you're a man you give advice
And you lie as though you've been there.

-D.G.

The Cost

My heart is too huge
And it hurts inside
The color of rouge,
With sorrow to guide,

Why am I here?
Should I even exist?
Although I hold dear,
Those who will be missed,

Where should I love?
Lost in a game,
My soul from above,
Shall never be tame,

A purposeless course,
Is not one to live,
In constant remorse,
Having all to give,

To merely exist,
And waiting to die,
A painful twist,
And a cause to cry,

Where is my breath?
I'm so very lost,
Considering death,
Consider the cost.

-M.J.

Sonnet III

Fore'er the cold of rock and stone bewitch,
That men will hunger for riches and wiles,
But finding scarce the gold and silver which
Feeds their lust and often twists them their smiles.
Each man and monster loses sight of rocks,
And fuel and fire become the instrument
That burns the heart, and at devil's door knocks
Berating lower men who, weak, seem bent.
But I who hid from heat and all the light
And in the dark have waited for relief
From burning sun and men that always fight
For who with power, power shall bequeath.
In your eyes, I have found the sapphires gone,
Relief from fire, while all the flame burns on.

-D.G.

Fall of a Monarch

I am a thief,
I am a liar,
I am your slave,
You are my sire,

Envy within,
Serving your whim,
You, I despise,
You, who will die,

You, I betray,
The serving I loathe,
Years gone astray,
Conspiring to choke,

Now in my hands,
You now understand,
Your corrupting ways,
Have ended your days.

-M.J.

Sonnet V

A scum beplagues the earth like a mucus
And fills all with an itch and scrape upon
The flesh, our land, and lay a stench on us
That make each mortal wish the rest were gone.
Through selfish deeds, the rot can only take
From honest men, whom break their back with sweat
And, slaving just to live, they their hearts doth break.
Oh scum! You are a vestige of regret.
Your mothers in their holy end would curse
If they could see the gutted stench and scar.
You sons of scum, they'd groan belitt'lings terse
And wish to be damned, for what you are.
Know this. Though you are pleased with self, you're ill,
And a day will be when the cure's to kill.

-D.G.

The Reviled Man

He sits alone,
The disposable man,
He lives on the streets,
Cursed & damned,

This homeless man,
Dirty & weary,
Has forgotten a life,
Drunk & dreary,

Frowned upon,
Living so low,
Living so wrong,
And dying too slow,

Unnoticed, unseen,
People walk nigh,
He wants to scream,
But they pass him by,

Hollow & gone,
He sits on the street,
Drunk & withdrawn,
And passed out asleep.

-M.J.

Mind, Body, & Troll

"Oh, my vision! My sight!
Get out of this place!
Get out of daylight,
With that hideous face!"

Said a man on the street,
To another he passed,
From his head to his feet,
His insults amassed,

"Well, that was quite rude,"
The ugly man spoke,
"But at least I'm not crude,
To some random ol' bloke!"

"You're an orc, and a liar!"
His rudeness declared,
"A foul troll lit on fire!"
Said he, who compared,

"Tis not what's in sight,
That makes someone foul,
Your shit words just might,
For your mind is a bowel!"

The rude man he huffed,
In defeat he was found,
'Cause his ego was scuffed,
As a crowd gathered 'round,

It was then that he learned,
It was he who was nasty.
The tables had turned,
His face became ghastly,

The crowd was repulsed,
At the sight of the beast,
But not from the troll,
Nay, not in the least.

The troll, now handsome,
He learned his own lesson,
And he now passed it on,
To the rude man in question.

-M.J.

Beheaded

'Beheader, Beheader!
Off with his head!
He's mocked the Queen,
So, he should be dead! '

'But M'Lord, M'Sire,
He said not a word,
He merely coughed,
That's all she heard! '

'I am the king,
I make the rules,
So cut off his head,
You hideous fool! '

The king's mistake,
What did him in,
His swollen ego,
That lies within,

The angry beheader,
The one who is armed,
Is never told off,
So he was alarmed,

He grabbed the king,
Threw him down,
Whacked off his head,
And stole his crown,

So don't be a snob,
To those who are less,
For y'might end up,
In a bloody mess.

-M.J.

Here I Lie

Silence a river, that endlessly flows,
Shattered to pieces, but nobody knows.
Nothing is left of the body that broke.
Twisted and broken, alone here I lie.

Sunlight that pierces the dark and the shade,
Down through the grate to the place where I laid.
Lights in the shadows, the stars in my night,
Twisted and broken, alone here I lie.

Metal that jingles and sways in the wind,
Taking my spirit from where it begins.
Scraping the stone like a sonnet that sings.
Twisted and broken, alone here I lie.

Turning the key of my neverness dream,
Burning my eyes in a silvery scream,
Churning the stomach and parting the flesh,
Twisted and broken, alone here I lie.

-D.G.

Life Support

They traveled abroad,
Mistakes were made,
Stuck in the snow,
Becoming afraid,

Time had passed,
The food was gone,
Desperate & crazed,
Survival was on,

Some were alive,
But most had died,
Aching for food,
The dead nearby,

Their only choice,
Their last resort,
To eat the dead,
For life support,

Eating so fresh,
A meal so hearty,
Tasting the flesh,
The Donner Party.

-M.J.

Indistinct

On a cold day in December,
I remember it quite clearly.
The snow was almost melted down.
Not all the way, but nearly.

As I was walking down the way,
I saw something, I think.
A block away, my eye was caught
by something indistinct.

It was in a kind of somewhat shape.
All sort of, you know... there.
I almost kept on walking by.
I almost didn't care.

However, I stepped closer
And I took a closer gander.
My curiosity was strong.
I had to play the pander.

It was so blurry, dark and dim,
So fuzzy, faint and hazy.
And yet I stepped up closer still.
I thought that I was crazy.

I thought it might have been my dream,
Or maybe aspirations.
It could have been my nightmare,
For it caused exacerbation.

It could have been a cloud of smoke
Left over from a joint.
It could have been that thought I'd had.
It could have been "The Point."

It could have been my hopes and dreams
That wavered there discreetly.
It could have been the life I missed.
Well, almost. Not completely.

I shook my fist. I stood and prayed.
I asked what it was there for,
This cloud of inconsistency
I simply didn't care for.

And as I prayed the wind picked up.
It blew hard and insistently.
I blinked but once, and as I blinked
It disappeared most instantly.

I thought that was the end of what
I'd never see again.
My hopes or dreams, some smoke or screams.
They were gone, but then…

The next day as I padded out
Across the road, you see,
The wisp I saw appeared again.
The time was half past three.

It wavered there in someone's yard
So innocent and clear.
I wanted just to run away.
Instead, I trotted near.

I whispered to it. "Go away.
I'm leaving you behind.
You cloud of indistinctliness,
Get lost, and ease my mind."

But never did it disappear.
It stood and simply wavered.
I took a step to walk away,
But then my courage quavered.

It floated right behind me,
Just a step or two in stride.
I ran and ran, but there it was.
"Please, go away!" I cried.

It followed me for days and weeks.
For months and years, you see.
I lost it for a day or two.
I knew that I was free.

Or so I thought, but in the night
I woke from sleep and screamed.
It stood above me on the bed,
Just like a cloud of steam.

"I'm part of you." It whimpered back.
"Oh no, you're not!" I cried.
I wanted bad to throttle it,
But then my anger died.

It dawned on me just what it was.
It was not things I say or think.
'Twas all the things that made me up.

'Twas something indistinct.

-D.G.

Prayer

Speak,
With the words God has given you,
As spoken before and will again,
That your soul may ignite
And be a lantern in this world.
Speak silently those words
That they fall gently in the wind.
Each word in eternity echoes,
Resonating,
Until each ripple grows and shakes and builds
Into a roaring cacophony that rumbles in the bones
And sings softly upon the heart.
How can such harmony help
But to tremble in the deep and crumble the mighty peaks
And raise the masses into a resounding shout
"Hallelujah!"
Speak, my friend,
Though the melody seems to fade,
For it will linger in its time,
And whether hidden or seen,
Will gather you home,
Though you may have lost your way.
Speak, dear soul
For God has given you voice.

-D.G.

Dear Sam

Don't you close your eyes, Dear Samuel.
Keep them open, don't be scared.
There's a world out there just waiting
And you'll need to be prepared.
There's a whole wide world of colors
and a universe of joy.
When you're laughing and you're playing
The whole world can be your toy.
And even though sometimes we cry
or run away in fear,
Just know that all things pass in time,
except what we hold dear.
Be strong, and do not fear, Dear Sam,
the monsters neath your bed,
or the shadows at your windows,
or the thoughts within your head.
It won't matter if you stumble
or fall down and have to crawl.
There's a love waiting to help you up
Until you're standing tall.
There's a family who loves you
and there's hundreds more who care.
Carry on, grow big and strong, Dear Sam
and you'll go most anywhere.

-D.G.

The Rat

The rat is nimble,
The rat is quick,
A snitch's symbol,
The rat sure is,

Evil doings,
The rat's plans,
Wicked grinning,
Rubbing hands,

Drooling tongue,
Desiring taste,
Motivation smug,
Making haste,

Grabbing a toe,
The man asleep,
Insatiable hunger,
The rat will reap,

Beware at night,
The rat will come,
Out of sight,
Preferring a thumb.

-M.J.

Lost Caws

High up in a tower,
She's filled with woe,
A girl inside dwells,
And she wishes to go,

Lamenting, she'll sigh,
For help with her plight,
When a crow, landing nigh,
Had gave her a fright,

'Oh! Hello Mr. Crow,
You gave me a scare,
What's brought ye here?'
She sought for his care,

She says 'To die alone,
It seems is my fate,
How I'm starving to bone,
Oh, how empty, my plate!'

The crow then speaks,
"Before you are deader",
He squawkingly shrieks,
"I'm to give you this letter!"

"It is one for reprieve,
Please, girl, do not cry,
For within is relief,
You will surely not die!'

"For the letter it reads:
'Your sentence revoked,
You're blameless of deeds,'"
At this, she seemed stoked!

"How I gleefully smile,
For I'm set to be free!
It's been a long while!
Why, decades for me!"

The crow had then spotted,
On the back of the note,
His stomach turned knotted,
And he said, (and I quote)

"Um, wait...you must know!"
The crow cawed out in shame,
He looked quite embarrassed,
"I've got the wrong name!"

"You had but one job!",
Cried out the crazed lass,
"You might want to leave,
Before I kicketh your ass!"

Quick to be flapping,
And away, he took flight,
Away from her madness,
To turn wrong into right.

-M.J.

I, the Raven

I, the raven, black and bleeding,
Though my life is now receding,
My life's story am I weaving
In this simple song of lore.

Back before my feathers wilted,
Black the night and sky so tilted,
Black was shadow wilted, on a dreary night so cold.

In the trees and leaves unshaken,
Sharply I became awakened
By some spirit old now aching,
Dream was breaking, taking hold.

And I, the raven, wings unfold
Did scatter in the midnight bold.

In my fluttered feathered fury,
While the bark grew dull and blurry,
Suddenly, I saw the eerie
Mansion of a simple soul.
And I, the raven, to its door
A tapping did my beak, there, toll.

I cannot fathom what possessed me
Or which god's grip did arrest me.
I, the raven, tapped and tattered
On that eerie mansion door.
I, the raven, did implore.

Slow but sure the door was answered
By a voice so surely cancered.
Came the quick and sleepy sound, "sir,
Please forgive me, I implore."

While the raven, I, was tapping
Surely, this poor soul was napping,
Thus, my wings and feathers flapping
Fluttered from the mansion door.
Why the fright, I was not sure.

Once the door it started ope'ning,
Once the man appeared, 'twas croaking
And the only thing then spoken
Was the single word, "Lenore…"
Only that and nothing more.

As inside, he then receded,
To the window, fast I heeded.
Hot my heart, entreated by that single word
"Lenore."

All at once a memory shuddered,
Through my feathered bones it flooded,
On my mind it thudded, as a body on the floor.
I, the raven, swift and sure.

Once before, in autumn breezes,
In that mansion came the wheezes,
And the sickly coughs and sneezes
Of a woman white and cold.
From that house, she stumbled bold.

Through the garden, ardent ran she,

Through the garden, 'til she soundly
Came upon a damp and dreadful
Puddle full of muck and mold,
In the tears of autumn cold.

I, the raven, perched and preening,
Despair, I witnessed, quickly streaming.
As the woman started screaming,
In her sight, I flew before.

"Help me, raven, I am dying!"
Wept she, wailing, still and crying,
As she, on the cold ground lying,
Of my service, did implore.

In that autumn, frequent after,
There she came with hopeful laughter,
As my master she began to act,
As a lord, not lady pure.
Breaking heart, did I restore.

Slowly sweet revealed her core,
Through the company she bore,
And she came to tell me
Of my lady's name, Lenore.

I, the raven, company and servant evermore.

As December cold approached,
On the autumn, frost encroachéd
While I fed on roaches, my dear lady did not show.

I, the raven, of my lady's death, I came to know.

When my focus then returnéd

To his soul my sorrow burned.
As the raven, I was learnéd
Of the ash he came to morn.
I, the raven, saw him torn.

On that window pane I rapped
As before, my beak, I tapped,
Tapped to find my host so apt
To ope' the window near the door
For my saddened soul so poor.

In I stepped with stately manner,
Though my host did stop and stammer,
I, the raven, sad and poor.

Quickly then my feathers sputtered.
Through the air I flew and fluttered
To a pallid bust of Pallas,
Free of malice 'bove the door.
I, the raven, heart so sore.

Once upon the marbled sculpture
Perched above the lonely old sir,
'til, upon my name, his lonely lordship did implore.

I, the raven, answered only,
Simply "Nevermore."

Be it chance the only word I knew was
"Nevermore."

Once that single word was uttered,
My host, he stared and stamped and muttered.

All at once his heart did flutter
While he mumbled something more.

Hoping then I might confess it,
Of his wife and love posssesséd,
Prayed my word would learn of him
The lost love of Lenore.

While he babbled, I, the raven, answered
"Nevermore."

Suddenly, he started raving,
As if some new answer craving.
Was his dying soul worth saving
While he yelled with rough and roar?

Through his outburst, I, the raven answered
"Nevermore."

"Prophet!" then he screamed and shouted,
"Thing of evil! God, thee, doubted!"

I, the raven, perched on Pallas,
Heard malice in his great uproar.

All at once he ceased his shouting,
Always doubting, always doubting,
While my shadow cast about him,
Drowning light upon the floor.

Silence then, and nothing more.

Could I help this man unfeeling,
While his mind and soul were reeling?
Could I sit upon the marble head

Of Pallas 'bove his chamber door?
Stealing light and lamp and lover,
From his darkened manor floor.

I, the raven, can't restore.

Furious with fever, fumbled.
Through the air his bible tumbled.
Grabbing book and story from his bookcase of forgotten lore.
Squarely struck, I, the raven, fell onto the floor.

Claw and beak and feathers flying,
I, the raven, pained and dying,
Flew the eerie mansion, I, the raven,
From above the door,
Into night, forever more.

I, the raven, black and bleeding,
Though my life is now receding.
I, the raven, messenger, companion,
Living nevermore,
Will be nevermore.

-D.G.

Maddness and Danger

The life in this world,
Will take your mind, and your light,
The dark spills in you

                                They tear you down, heart and mind.
                                        Humanity is awful.

The mind is now lost,
Amidst the dreary prison
My shell, a relic

                                        The worst enemy within,
                                        Silence becomes a danger.

Sorrow will spin you
Where is reality now?
Laughing, it's absurd

                                        Painful conversations play,
                                        Looping over and over.

Results may vary,
And all results are futile,
Desperately tried,

                                        Convinced of resolution
                                        Upon ears too deaf to hear.

Offering your thoughts,
They seep out wrongly spoken,
Clarity is snuffed,

                                        All pleas withdrawn in the mind,

>   Goodwill becomes a madness.

The darkened bedrooms,
Ache in their walls, sobbing tears,
Discomfort the bed,

>   Empty brick halls, cold echoes,
>   A song of pain no one hears.

Clawing your thoughts out,
Bleeding ink onto paper,
They drip into words,

>   Words that cannot be erased,
>   Words that will not be ignored.

Capturing their eyes,
Branding their soul with your words,
Indomitable,

>   The art of words, your weapon,
>   Darkness, your sanctuary.

Defending wisdom,
Striking against ignorance,
Contrasted ink screams

>   Strength grows. Powerful. Stranger.
>   Our truth: Madness and Danger.

-M.J. & D.G.

End

About The Authors

Daniel Gerber is a strange man. A very strange man, indeed, but also a most accomplished man who happened to grow up in a normal, loving family in the southeastern corner of Washington State in a collection of cities referred to locally as the Tri-cities. He has always carried with him a strong passion for the arts that has especially flourished since his years in college, where he did his undergrad in Theatre Performance, and eventually achieved a Master's Degree in Business Administration. He now enjoys spending his free time having fun with his family, playing D&D, practicing archery and Kung Fu, as well as painting, and of course, writing, with his lady love.

He picked up art, poetry, and fiction writing during high school. Daniel is very ambitious and works fervently on his creations and projects, all of which reveal hidden notes of his honorable, yet eccentric, character and spirit. He has had his share of experiences from his lifelong battle with depression, bad relationships, and heartbreaks, to exploring deep thought and spirituality, and reflecting a whimsical humor during joyful times, which have all served as inspiration for his charming poetry.

In addition to his self-published works, "The Otherside Chronicles", "True Faith", and "The Misadventures of Snowball" (all are available on Amazon), he plans to continue writing many books, selling prints of his art, and assisting in refinishing furniture.

Maddy Jones also grew up in the Tri-cities. She endured multiple traumatizing events in her childhood and young adulthood, as well as toxic relationships, resulting in an anxiety disorder and major depressive disorder, which she has made remarkable progress with. She has always used visual arts and writing as an outlet of personal expression and creativity.

In spite of her past, Maddy has tremendous emotional intelligence and a strong empathic nature. Her circle of friends is enormous and extraordinary, though sometimes peculiar. Maddy's sense of humor is equally tremendous, and she delights in puns so bad they'll melt your eyebrows off. She's been into art and writing since early childhood, and happily dabbles in different mediums, styles and unusual concepts. She's also a damned fine cook.

She spent several years refinishing furniture as a stay-at-home mom through her own business, Paint Misbehavin', where she developed an impressive repertoire of ugly-turned-beautiful pieces.

Maddy has grown quickly in recent years to the point of collaborating on this book, the first printed edition of her poetry. Maddy's wonderful sense of humor, enjoyment of darker and macabre works, as well as her appreciation for the unusual and the strange, have given her creativity that inspires and delights. Maddy aspires to continue work in refinishing furniture, selling prints of her artwork, and enjoying the wondrous benefits of artistic projects continuing forward.

www.ingramcontent.com/pod-product-compliance
Lightning Source LLC
Chambersburg PA
CBHW072335300426
44109CB00042B/1628